Piano • Vocal • Guitar

BEST OF
THE LOVIN' SPOONFUL
PLUS OTHER HITS BY JOHN SEBASTIAN

T0070905

John Sebastian at 1970 Isle of Wight Music Festival –
photograph by Charles Everest – © www.CameronLife.co.uk

The Lovin' Spoonful – photograph by Henry Diltz

ISBN 978-1-4803-9664-7

HAL•LEONARD®
CORPORATION
7777 W. BLUEMOUND RD. P.O. BOX 13819 MILWAUKEE, WI 53213

In Australia Contact:
Hal Leonard Australia Pty. Ltd.
4 Lentara Court
Cheltenham, Victoria, 3192 Australia
Email: ausadmin@halleonard.com.au

Visit Hal Leonard Online at
www.halleonard.com

CONTENTS

4 Darling, Be Home Soon

11 Daydream

14 Did You Ever Have to Make Up Your Mind?

17 Do You Believe in Magic

20 I Had a Dream

26 Jug Band Music

30 Nashville Cats

35 Rain on the Roof

38 Rainbows All Over Your Blues

43 She's a Lady

46 Summer in the City

52 Welcome Back

49 You Didn't Have to Be So Nice

56 You're a Big Boy Now

60 Younger Girl

DARLING, BE HOME SOON

Words and Music by
JOHN SEBASTIAN

Come, ___ and

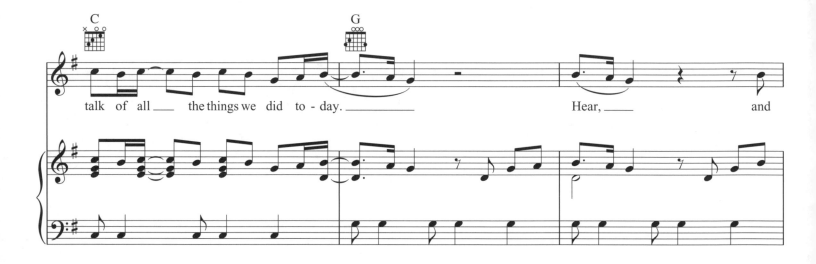

talk of all ___ the things we did to-day. _____ Hear, ___ and

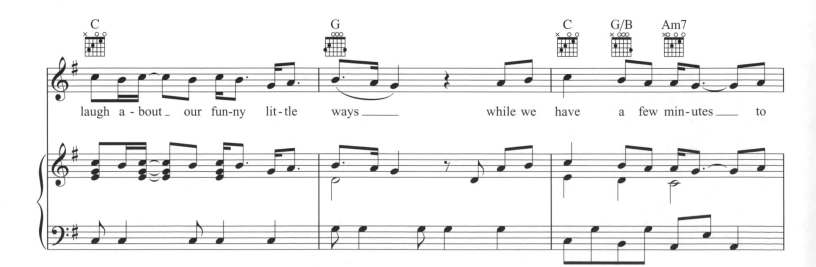

laugh a-bout ___ our fun-ny lit-tle ways _____ while we have a few min-utes ___ to

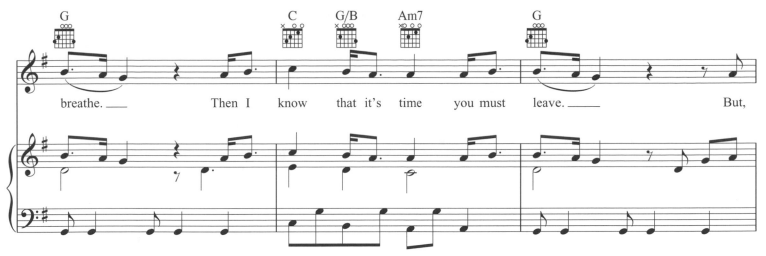

breathe. ____ Then I know that it's time you must leave. ____ But,

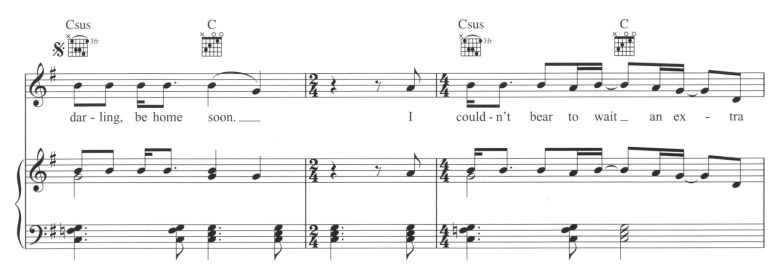

dar - ling, be home soon. ____ I could - n't bear to wait ___ an ex - tra

min - ute if you daw - dled. My dar - ling, be home soon. ____

It's not just these few hours, ___ but I've been wait - ing since I tod - dled

To Coda

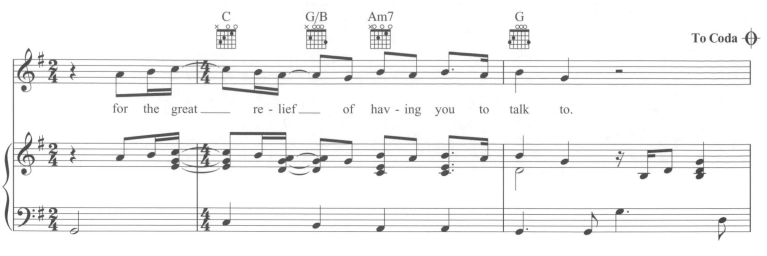

for the great _____ re - lief _____ of hav - ing you to talk to.

And now _____ a quar - ter of _____ my life is al - most

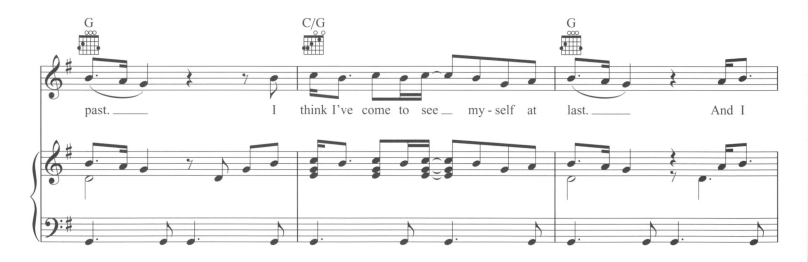

past. _____ I think I've come to see _____ my - self at last. _____ And I

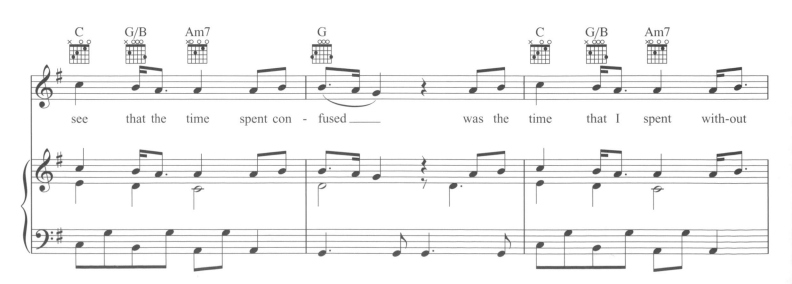

see that the time spent con - fused _____ was the time that I spent with-out

you. _____ And I feel my-self in bloom. _____

D.S. al Coda

CODA

So,

So, dar - ling, __ my dar - ling, be home soon. __

I could - n't bear to wait __ an ex - tra min - ute if you daw - dled.

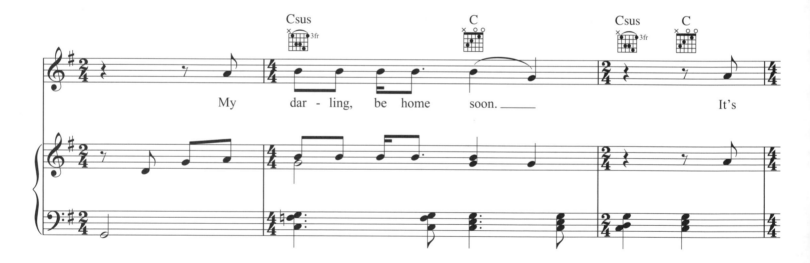

My dar - ling, be home soon. _____ It's

not just these few hours, __ but I've been wait - ing since I tod - dled for the great __

_____ re-lief _____ of hav-ing you to talk to.

Go _____ and beat your cra-zy head a-gainst _ the sky. _____

Try _____ and see be-yond _ the hous - es in your eyes. _____ It's o -

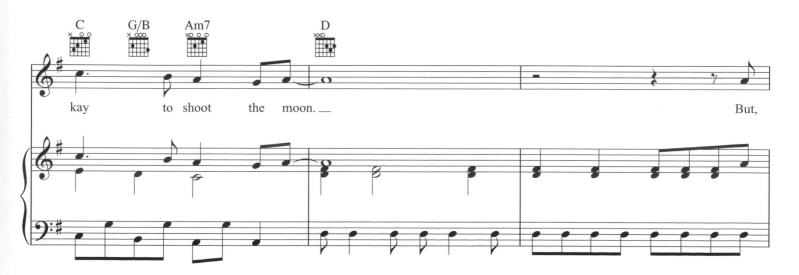

kay to shoot the moon. _ But,

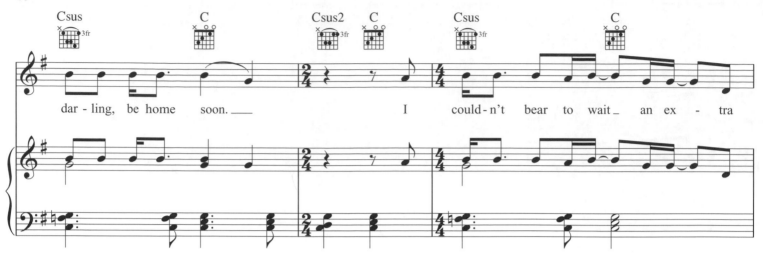

dar - ling, be home soon. ___ I could-n't bear to wait ___ an ex - tra

min - ute if you daw - dled. My dar - ling, be home soon. ___

It's not just these few hours, _ but I've been wait - ing since I tod - dled

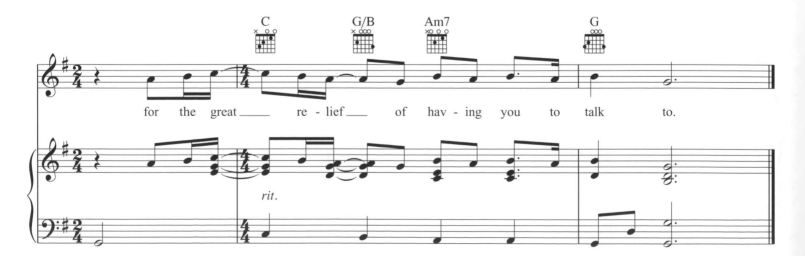

for the great ___ re - lief ___ of hav - ing you to talk to.

DAYDREAM

Words and Music by
JOHN SEBASTIAN

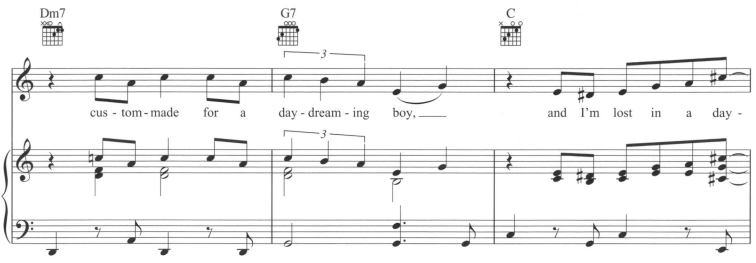

cus - tom - made for a day - dream - ing boy, ___ and I'm lost in a day -

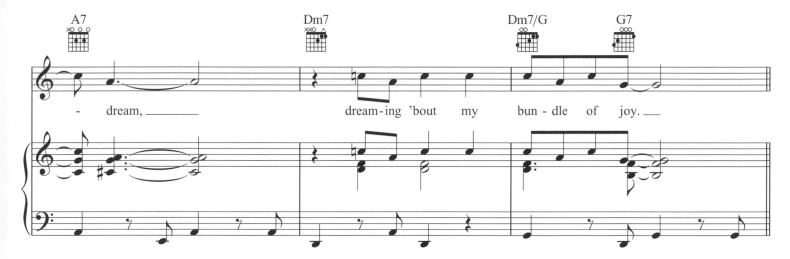

- dream, ___ dream-ing 'bout my bun - dle of joy. ___

Repeat and Fade

Whistle

Optional Ending

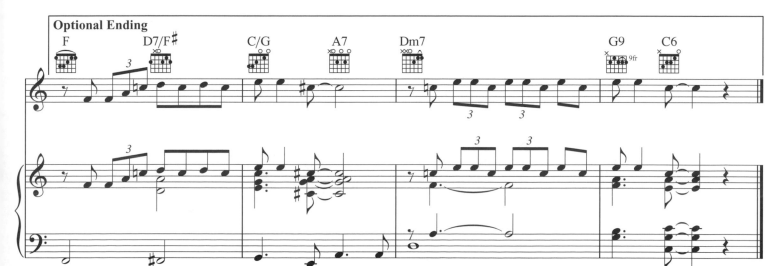

DID YOU EVER HAVE TO MAKE UP YOUR MIND?

Words and Music by
JOHN SEBASTIAN

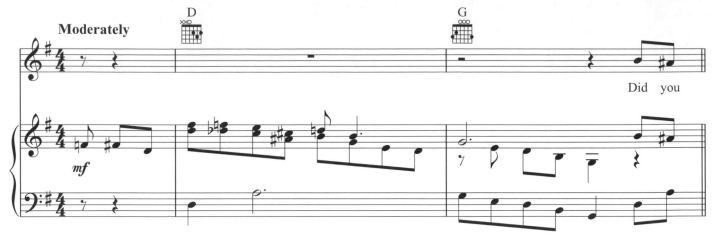

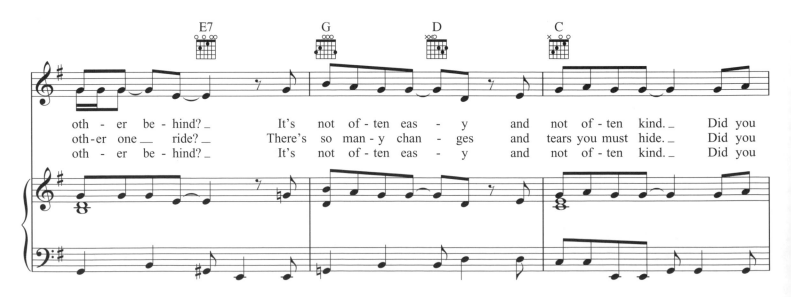

D.S. al Coda

mou - sy lit - tle girl. And then you

CODA

bet - ter go home, son, and

make up your mind." Then you bet you bet - ter fi - n'lly de - cide ____ and

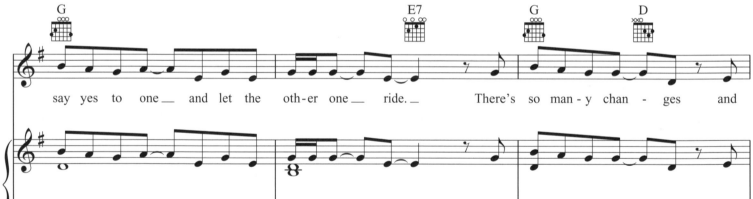

say yes to one ___ and let the oth - er one ___ ride. ___ There's so man - y chan - ges and

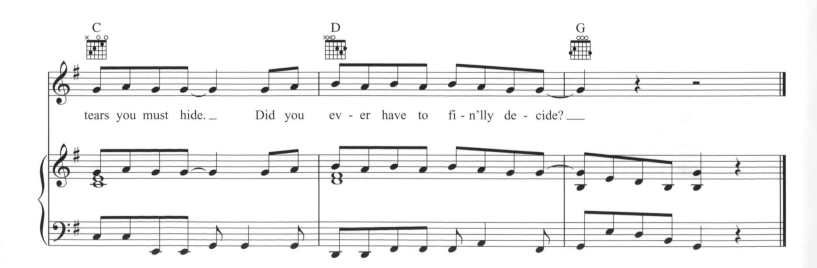

tears you must hide. ___ Did you ev - er have to fi - n'lly de - cide? ___

DO YOU BELIEVE IN MAGIC

Words and Music by
JOHN SEBASTIAN

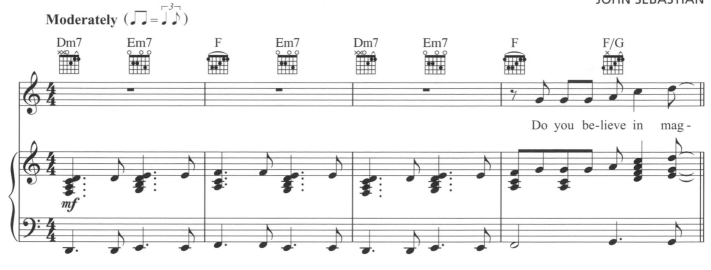

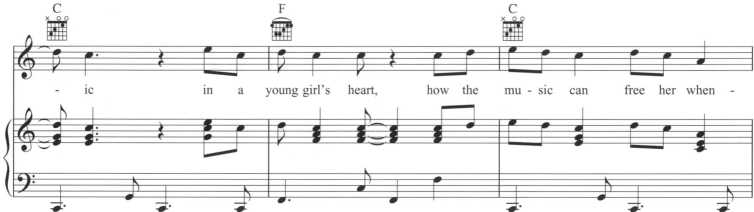

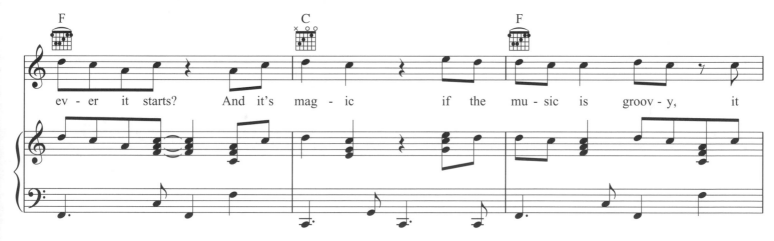

free your soul, but it's like try-in' to tell a stran-ger 'bout a rock and roll. ____

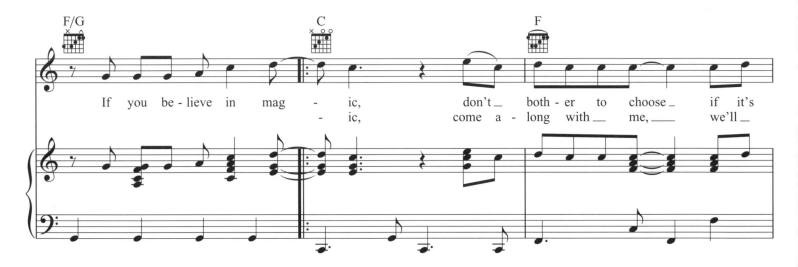

If you be-lieve in mag - ic, don't __ both-er to choose __ if it's
- ic, come a - long with __ me, ____ we'll __

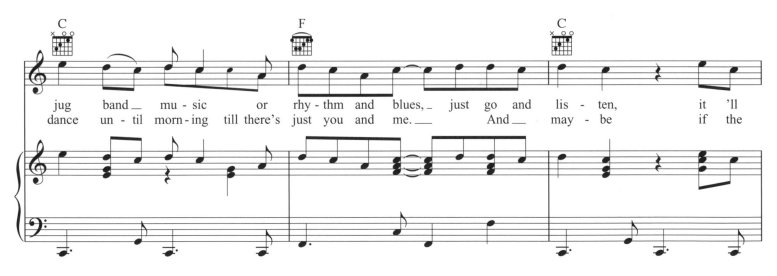

jug band __ mu - sic or rhy - thm and blues, __ just go and lis - ten, it 'll
dance un - til morn-ing till there's just you and me. __ And __ may - be if the

start with a smile that won't wipe off your face no mat - ter how hard you try. Your
mu - sic is right, I'll __ meet you to-mor - row sort of late ____ at night. And

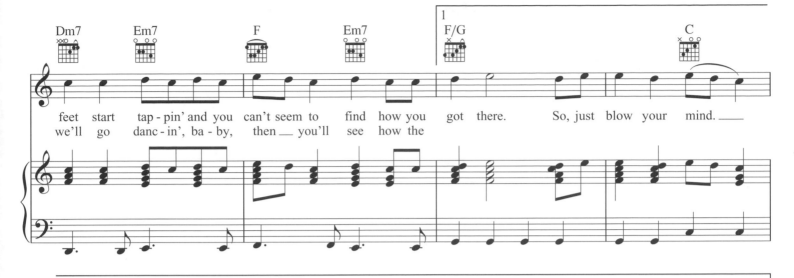

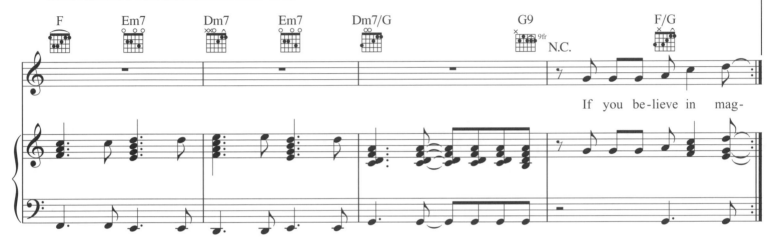

I HAD A DREAM

Words and Music by
JOHN SEBASTIAN

I _____ had a dream last night.

What a love-ly dream it was. ___

I _____ dreamed we all ___ were al - right,

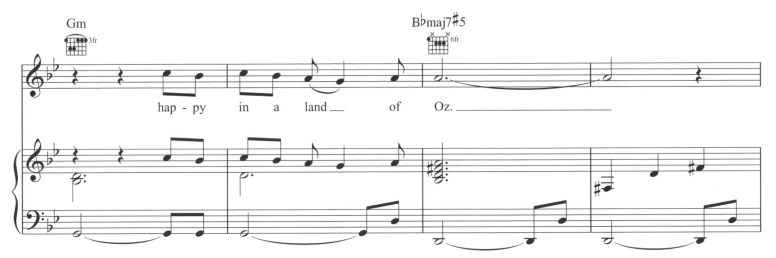

hap - py in a land __ of Oz. _____

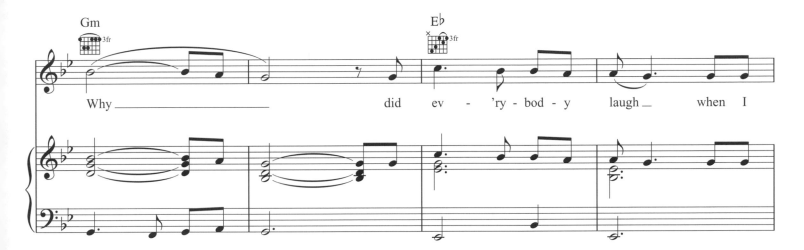

Why _____ did ev - 'ry - bod - y laugh __ when I

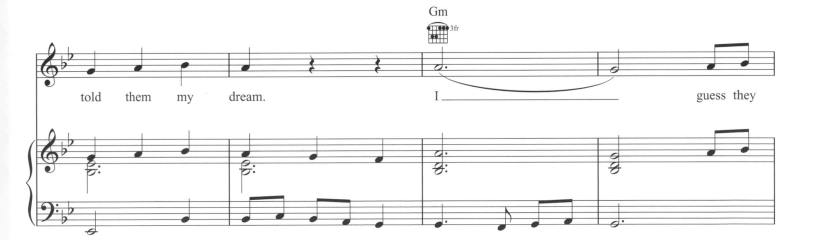

told them my dream. I _____ guess they

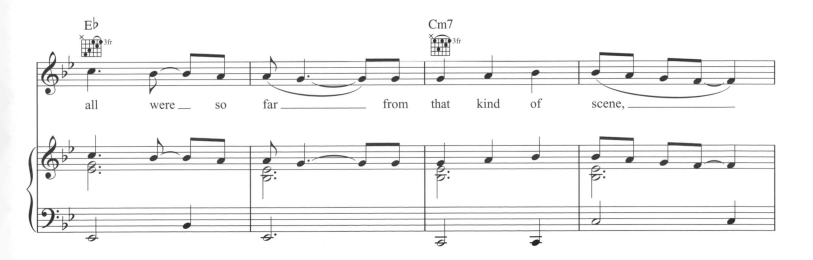

all were __ so far _____ from that kind of scene, _____

feel - in' mean. ___

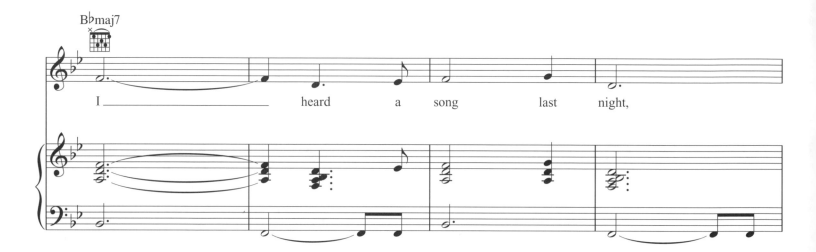

I ___ heard a song last night,

what a love - ly song it was. ___

I thought I'd hum it all night. Un - for -

get - ta - ble ___ be - cause _____ all of the

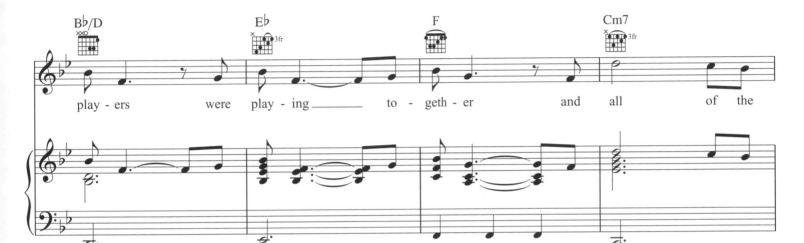

play - ers were play - ing _____ to - geth - er and all of the

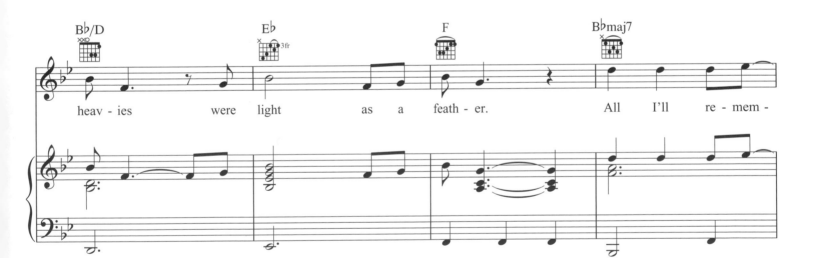

heav - ies were light as a feath - er. All I'll re - mem -

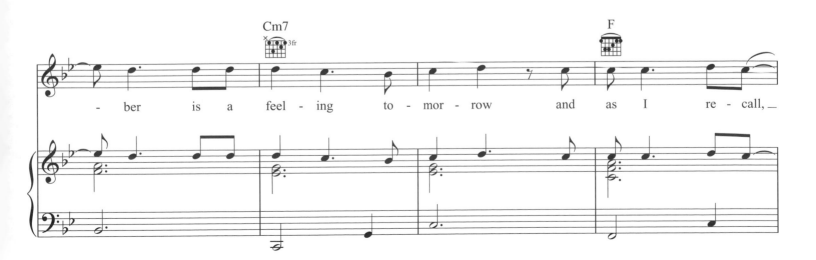

- ber is a feel - ing to - mor - row and as I re - call, __

the rest will just fol - low.

I _____ had a dream last night.

What a love - ly dream it was. ____

I dreamed we all ____ were al - right,

hap - py in a land — of Oz. _____

Optional Ending

Repeat and Fade

JUG BAND MUSIC

Words and Music by
JOHN SEBASTIAN

Lyrics:

I was down in Sa-van-nah, eat-in' cream and ba-na-nas when the heat just made me faint. ___ I be-gan to get cross-eyed, I thought I was lost, ___ I'd be-gun to see ___ things as they ain't. ___ As the

So, if you ev-er get sick-ly, get sis to run quick-ly to the dust-y clos-et shelf ___ and pull down a wash-board and play a gui-tar ___ chord and do a lit-tle "do-it-your-self." ___

rel - a - tives gath - ered to see what's the mat - ter, the doc - tor came to see was I dyin'. __
Call on your neigh - bors to put down their la - bors and come and play the hard-ware in time, __

D7 C

__ But the doc - tor said, __ "Give him jug band __ mu - sic, it
__ 'cause the doc - tor said, __ "Give him jug band __ mu - sic, it

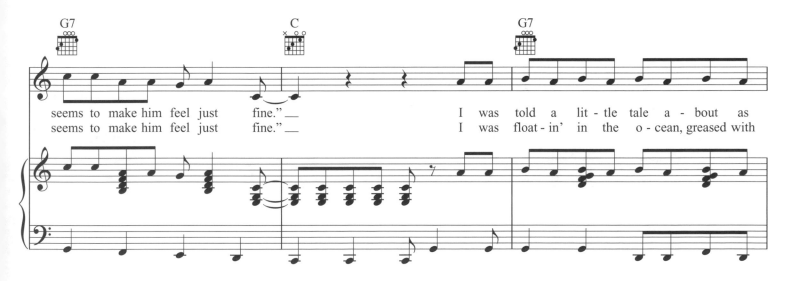

G7 C G7

seems to make him feel just fine." __ I was told a lit - tle tale a - bout as
seems to make him feel just fine." __ I was float - in' in the o - cean, greased with

C

skin - ny as a rail, eight - foot __ cow - boy __ with a head - ache. He was
sun - tan __ lo - tion, when I got wiped __ out by a beach - boy. He was

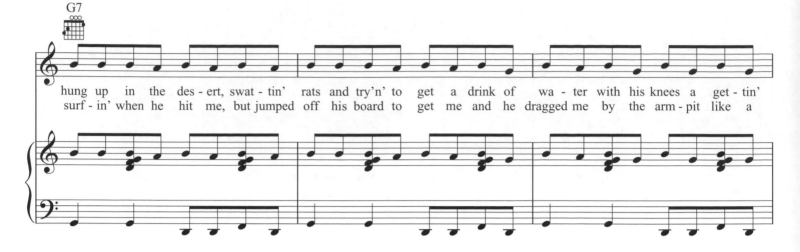

hung up in the des - ert, swat - tin' rats and try'n' to get a drink of wa - ter with his knees a get - tin'
surf - in' when he hit me, but jumped off his board to get me and he dragged me by the arm - pit like a

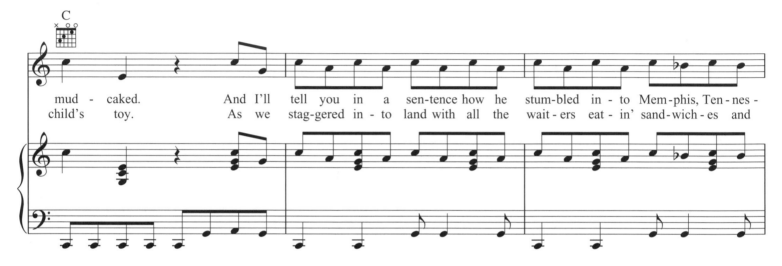

mud - caked. And I'll tell you in a sen - tence how he stum - bled in - to Mem - phis, Ten - nes -
child's toy. As we stag - gered in - to land with all the wait - ers eat - in' sand - wich - es and

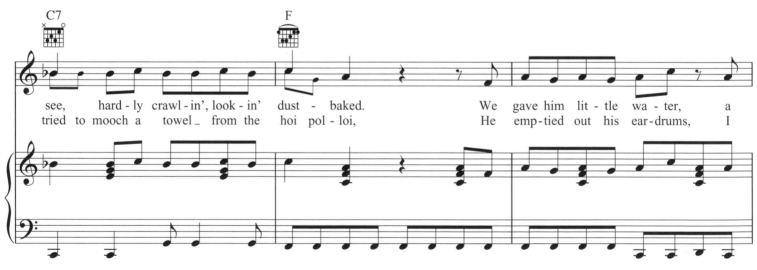

see, hard - ly crawl - in', look - in' dust - baked. We gave him lit - tle wa - ter, a
tried to mooch a towel _ from the hoi pol - loi, He emp - tied out his ear - drums, I

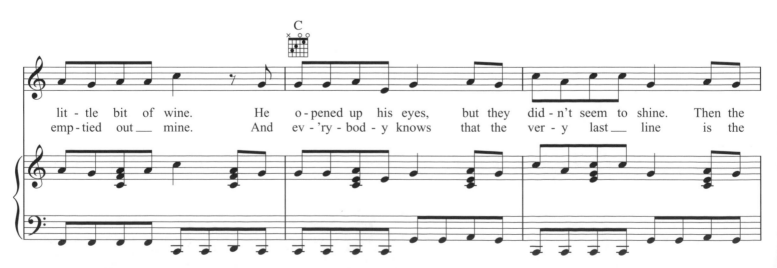

lit - tle bit of wine. He o - pened up his eyes, but they did - n't seem to shine. Then the
emp - tied out __ mine. And ev - 'ry - bod - y knows that the ver - y last __ line is the

doc - tor said, __ "Give him jug band __ mu - sic, it seems to make him feel just fine." _
doc - tor said, __ "Give him jug band __ mu - sic, it seems to make him feel just fine." _

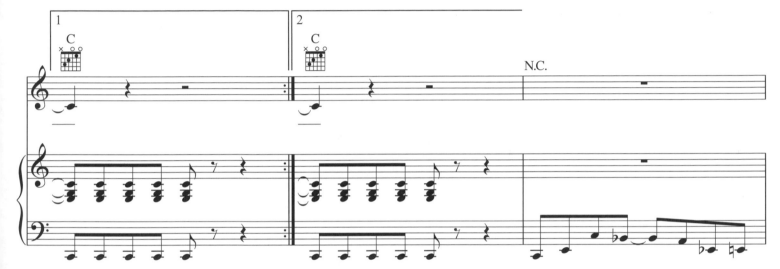

And the doc - tor said, __ "Give him jug band __ mu - sic, it

seems to make him feel just fine." _____

NASHVILLE CATS

Words and Music by
JOHN SEBASTIAN

Brightly

Nash - ville Cats play clean as coun-try wa - ter.

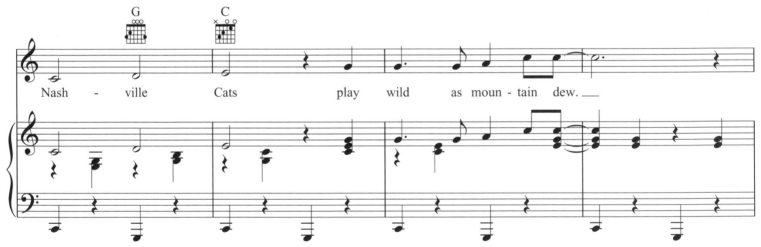

Nash - ville Cats play wild as moun-tain dew. ___

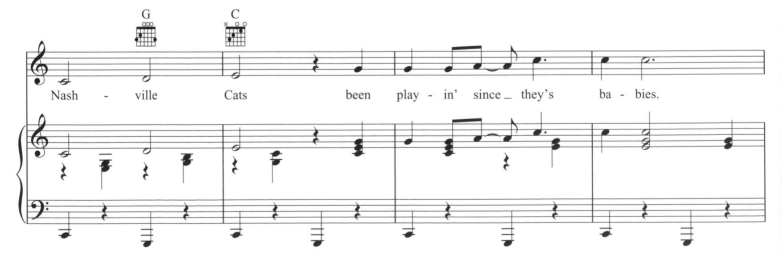

Nash - ville Cats been play-in' since ___ they's ba - bies.

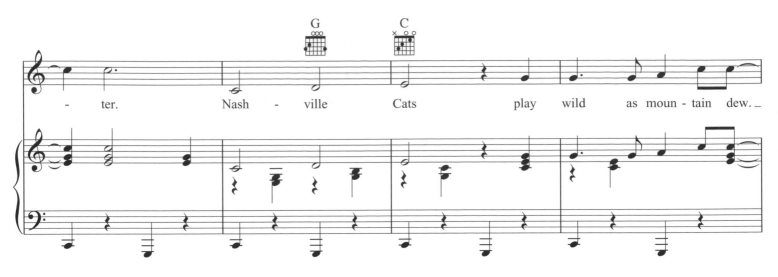

-ter. Nash - ville Cats play wild as moun - tain dew. __

Nash - ville Cats been

play - in' since __ they's ba - bies. Nash - ville

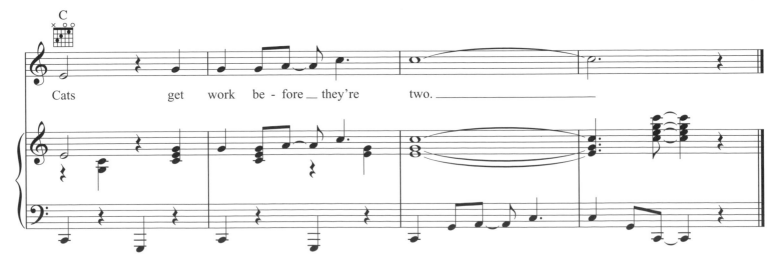

Cats get work be - fore __ they're two. __

RAIN ON THE ROOF

Words and Music by
JOHN SEBASTIAN

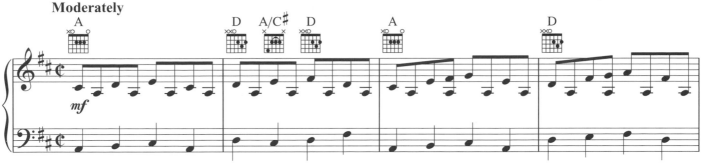

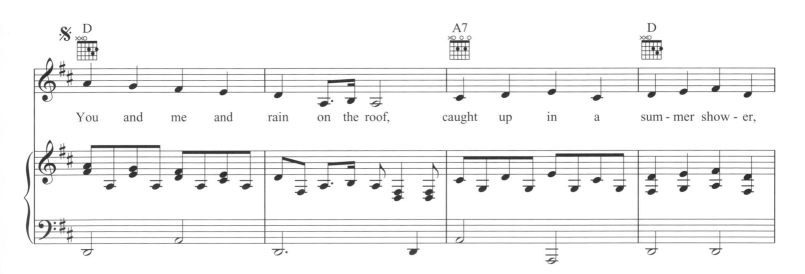

You and me and rain on the roof, caught up in a sum-mer show-er,

dry-ing while it soaks the flow-ers. May-be we'll be

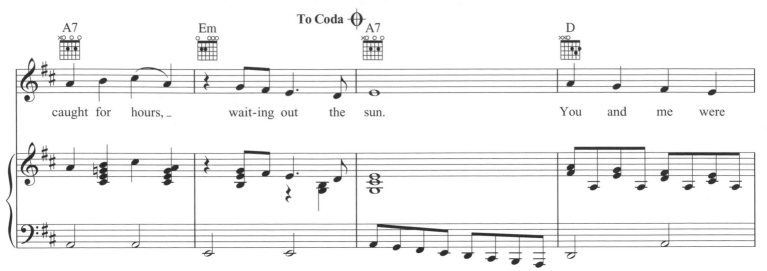

caught for hours, _ wait-ing out the sun. You and me were

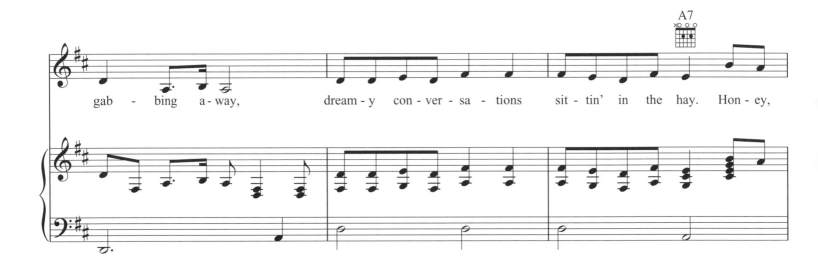

gab - bing a - way, dream - y con - ver - sa - tions sit - tin' in the hay. Hon - ey,

how long was I laugh-ing in the rain with you? 'Cause I did-n't feel a drop till the thun-der brought us to.

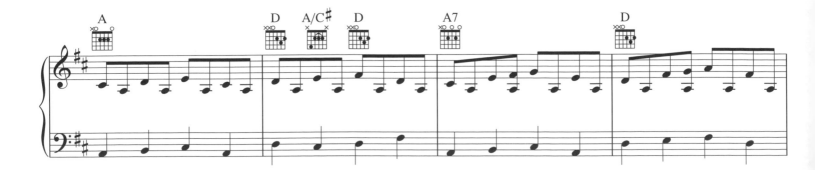

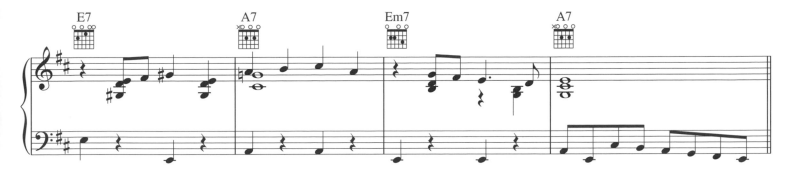

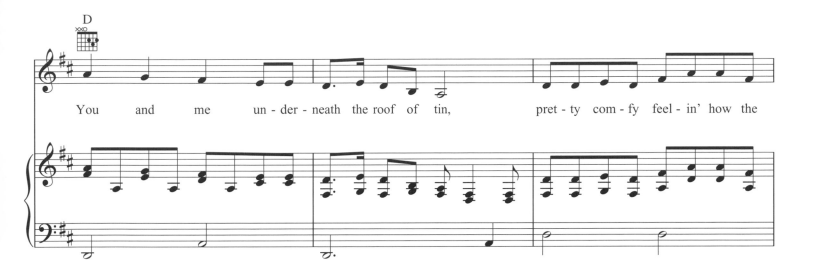

You and me un - der - neath the roof of tin, pret - ty com - fy feel - in' how the

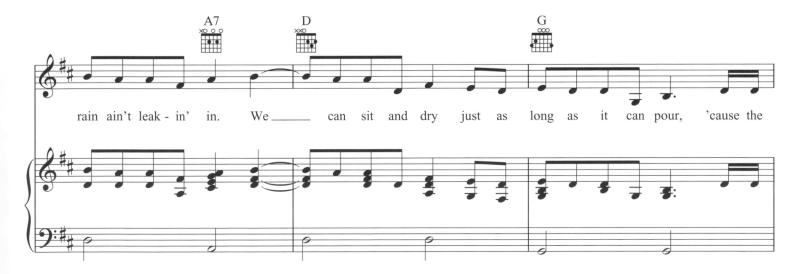

rain ain't leak - in' in. We _____ can sit and dry just as long as it can pour, 'cause the

D.S. al Coda

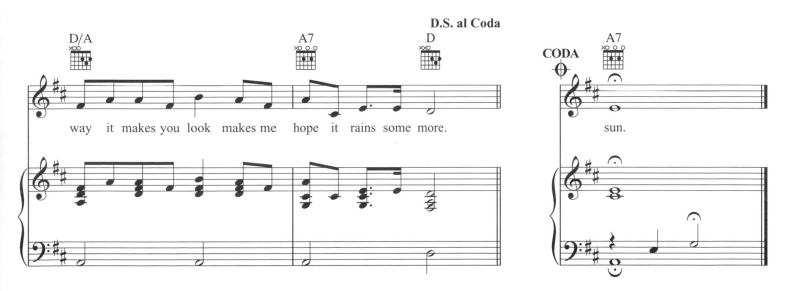

way it makes you look makes me hope it rains some more.

CODA

sun.

RAINBOWS ALL OVER YOUR BLUES

Words and Music by
JOHN SEBASTIAN

I been wait - in' my time _____ just to talk to you. _____

Instrumental solo ad lib.

_____ You've been look - in' all down _ in the mouth _

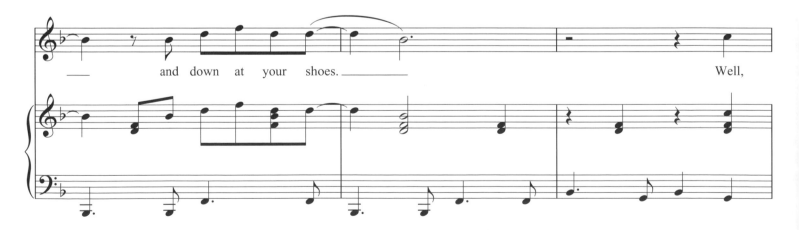

_____ and down at your shoes. _____ Well,

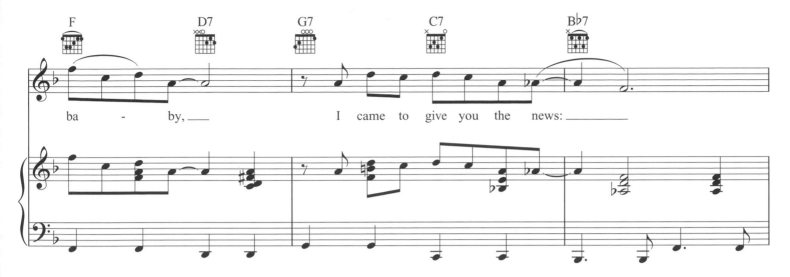

ba - by, ___ I came to give you the news: _____

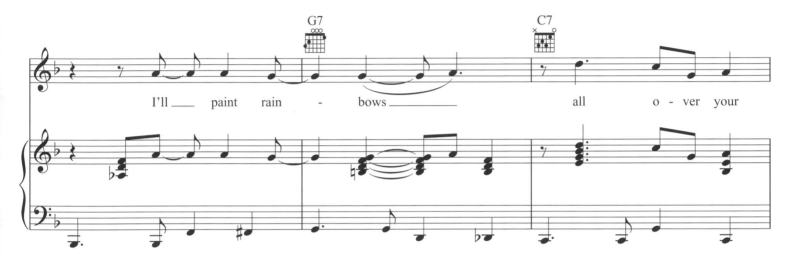

I'll ___ paint rain - bows _____ all o - ver your

To Coda ⊕

blues. _____ I heard you been spend - in' a lot of your time __

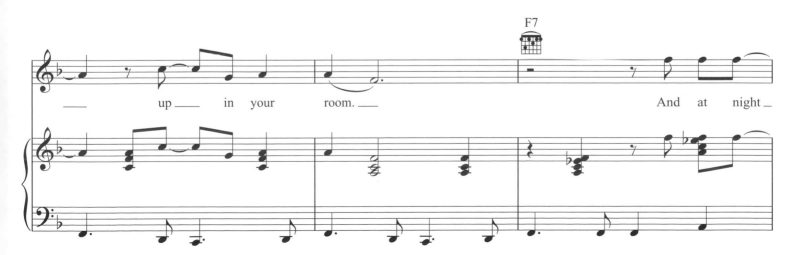

__ up __ in your room. __ And at night __

you been watch - in' _____ the dark side of the moon. _____

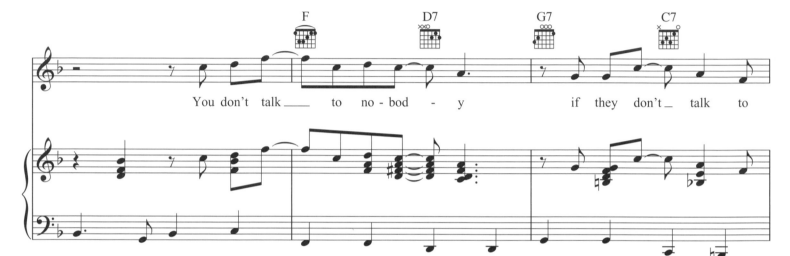

You don't talk _____ to no-bod — y _____ if they don't _ talk to

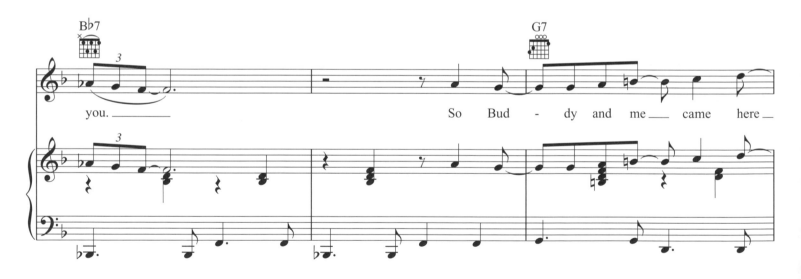

you. _____ So Bud — dy and me _ came here _____

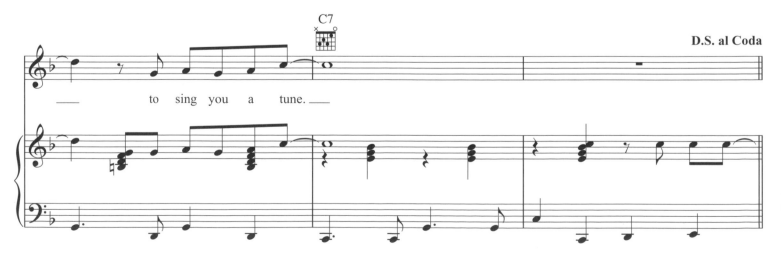

D.S. al Coda

_____ to sing you a tune. _____

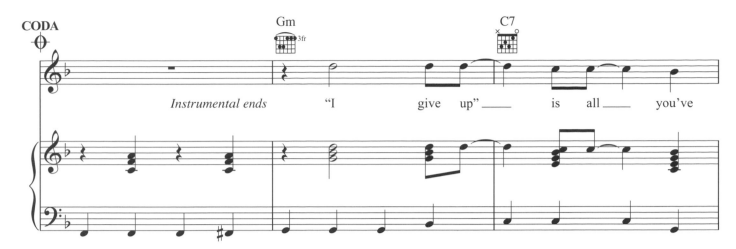

CODA

Instrumental ends   "I   give up" ____   is all ____   you've

real-ly   got   to   say. ____   It's   time ____   to   find ____   a   new ____   life-style   'cause

this   real-ly   ain't   the   way. ____   Let's   go ____   for   a   bounce ____

on   my   tram-po-line. ____   I   can   show ____   you   the   pret-ti-est   moun-

- tains that you've ev - er seen. _____ You bet - ter run to your

clos - et and fish out your blue suede shoes. __ I'll paint rain - bows _____

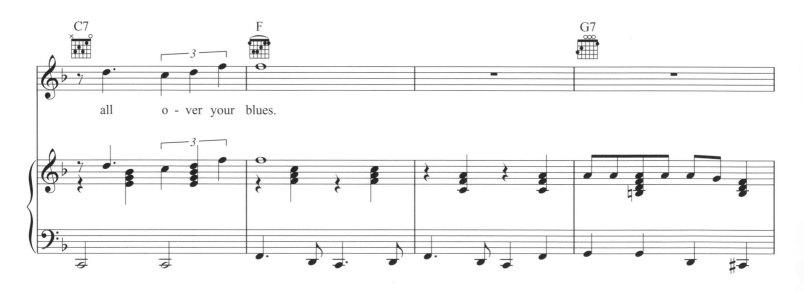

all o - ver your blues.

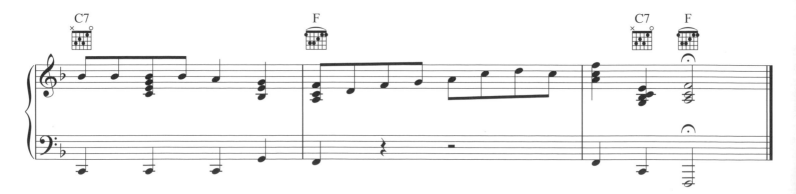

SHE'S A LADY

Words and Music by
JOHN SEBASTIAN

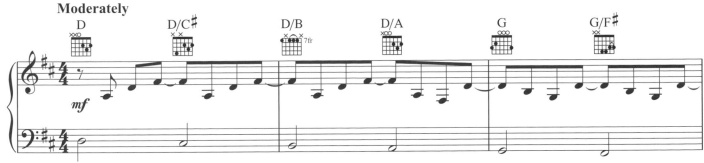

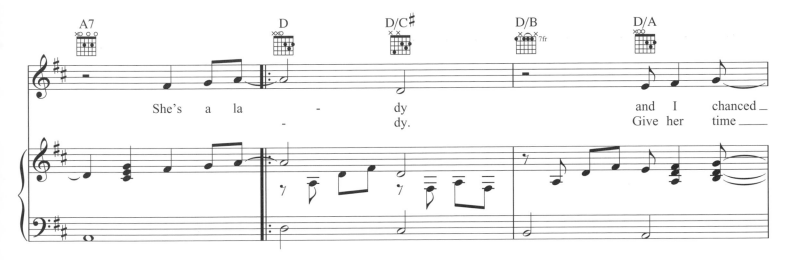

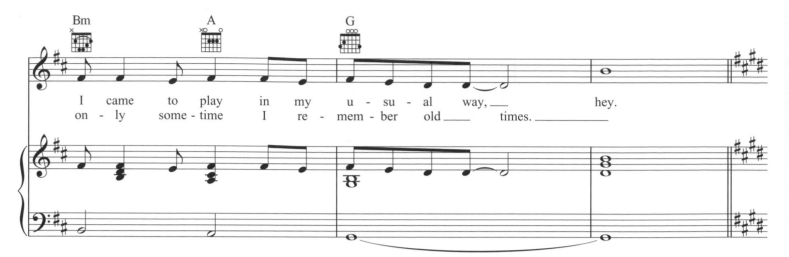

I came to play in my u - su - al way, ___ hey.
on - ly some - time I re - mem - ber old ___ times. ___

Float - ing a - long ___ with a whim - si - cal twink - ling in ___ her strange ___ green eyes. ___
And when she says, ___ "Can you guess? ___ It's a dress ___ you won't be - lieve. ___

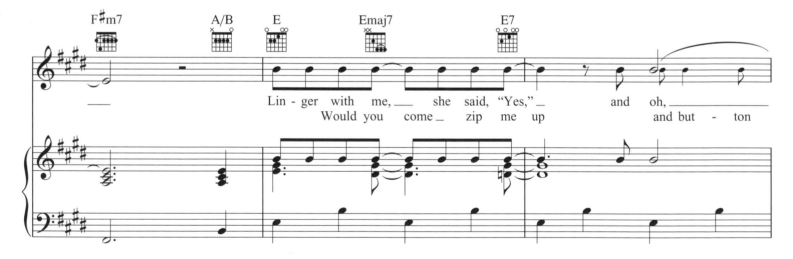

___ Lin - ger with me, ___ she said, "Yes," ___ and oh, ___
Would you come ___ zip me up ___ and but - ton

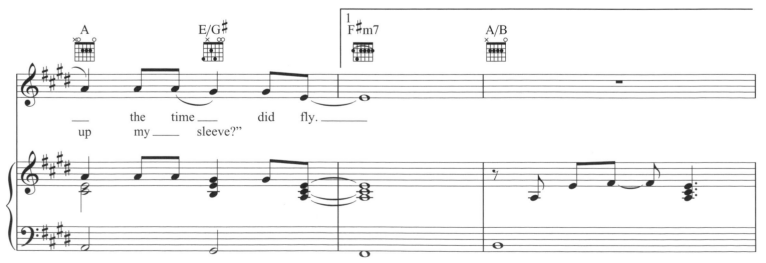

___ the time ___ did fly. ___
up my ___ sleeve?"

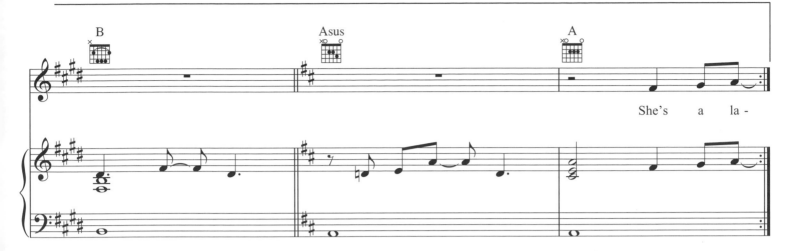

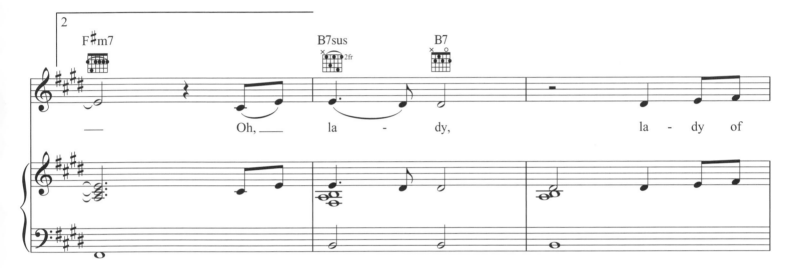

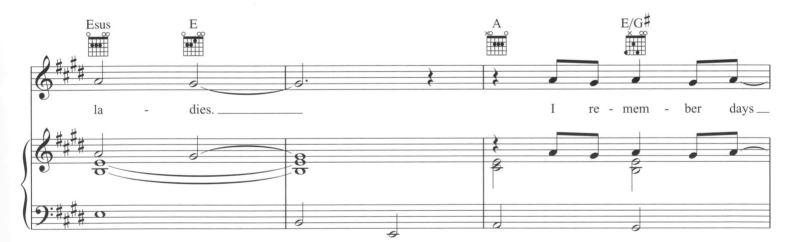

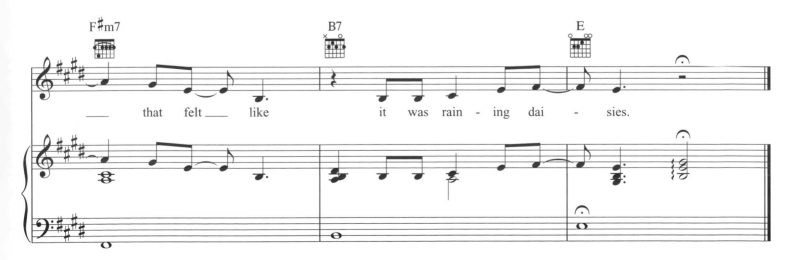

SUMMER IN THE CITY

Words and Music by JOHN SEBASTIAN,
STEVE BOONE and MARK SEBASTIAN

Moderately, with a steady beat

Instrumental to Fade

Hot town, sum-mer in the cit-y, back o' neck get-ting dirt-y and grit-ty.
Cool town, eve-nin' in the cit-y, dressed so fine and a-look-in' so pret-ty.

Been down, is-n't it a pit-y? Does-n't seem to be a shad-ow in the cit-y.
Cool cat, look-in' for a kit-ty. Gon-na look in ev-'ry cor-ner of the cit-y.

All a-round, peo-ple look-in' half dead, walk-in' on the side-walk hot-ter than a match-head.
Till I'm wheez-in' like a bus stop, run-nin' up the stairs, gon-na meet you on the roof-top.

But at night it's a dif-f'rent world, __

go out and find a girl. __ Come on, come on and dance __ all night, __

de-spite the heat it-'ll be al-right. __ And, babe, don't you know it's a pit-y the

days can't be like the nights, in the sum-mer __ in the cit-y, __ in the

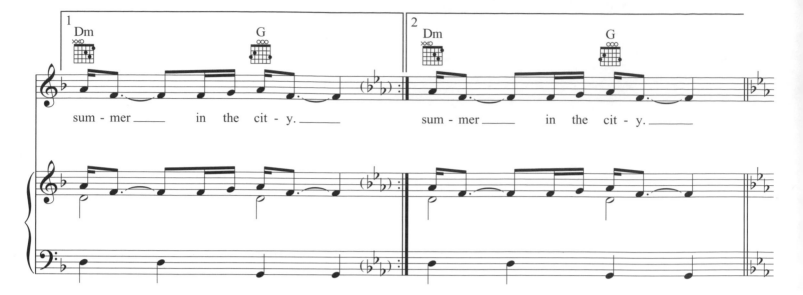

sum - mer _____ in the cit - y. _____   sum - mer _____ in the cit - y. _____

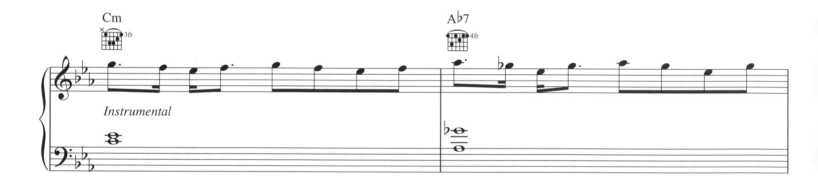

Instrumental

D.S. and Fade
(Instrumental)

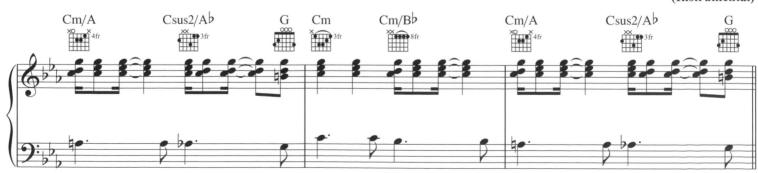

YOU DIDN'T HAVE TO BE SO NICE

Words and Music by JOHN SEBASTIAN
and STEVE BOONE

Moderately fast

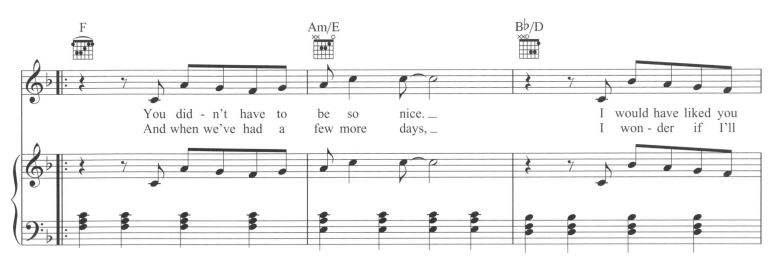

You did-n't have to be so nice. ___ I would have liked you
And when we've had a few more days, ___ I won-der if I'll

an-y - way, ___ if you had just looked once or twice ___
get to say, ___ "You did-n't have to be so nice, ___

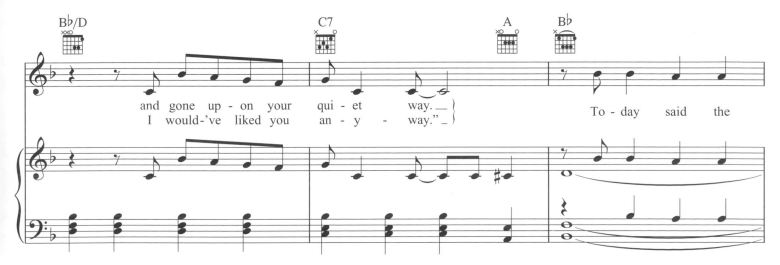

and gone up-on your qui-et way. ___ To-day said the
I would-'ve liked you an-y - way." ___

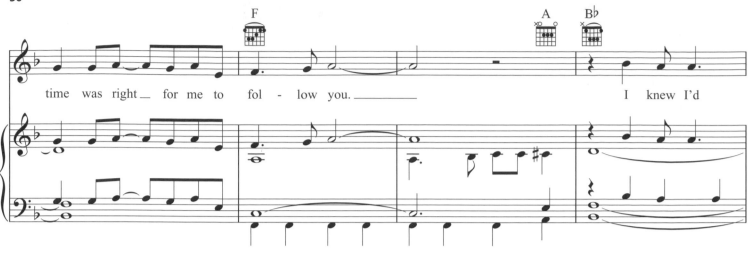

time was right __ for me to fol - low you. _____ I knew I'd

find you in a day or two and it's true.

{ You came up - on a
{ You did - n't have to

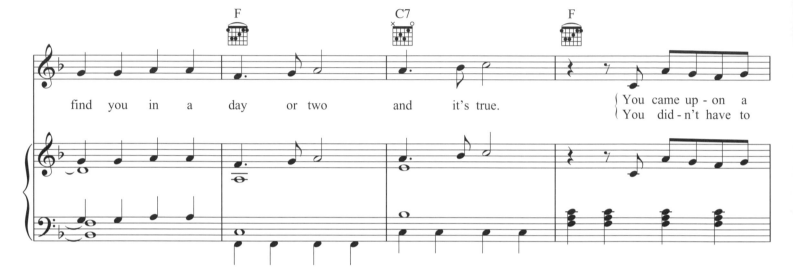

qui - et day. __
be so nice. __

You sim - ply seemed to take your place. __
I would have liked you an - y - way, __

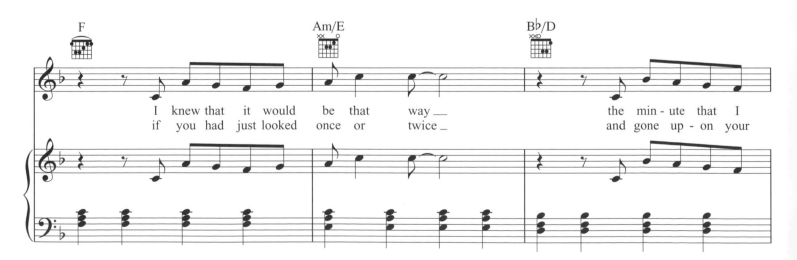

I knew that it would be that way __
if you had just looked once or twice __

the min - ute that I
and gone up - on your

WELCOME BACK

Words and Music by
JOHN SEBASTIAN

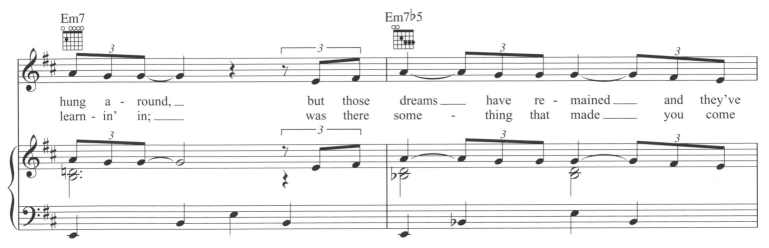

hung a - round, __ but those dreams __ have re - mained __ and they've
learn - in' in; __ was there some - thing that made __ you come

turned a - round. __ Who'd __ have thought they'd lead ya
back a - gain? __ And what __ could ev - er lead ya

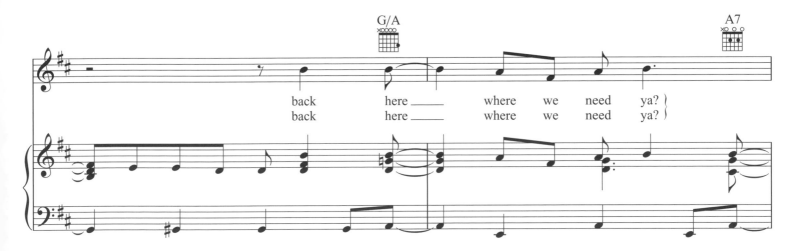

back here __ where we need ya?
back here __ where we need ya?

Yeah, we tease him a lot __ 'cause we got

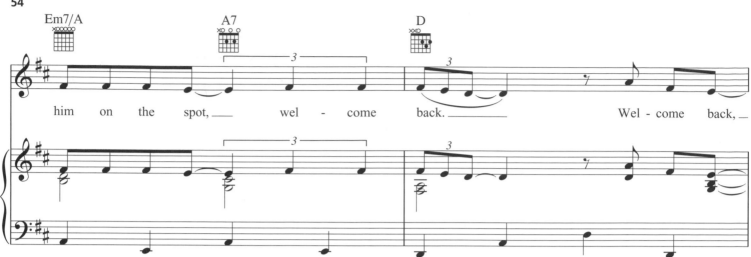

him on the spot, ____ wel - come back. _____ Wel - come back, __

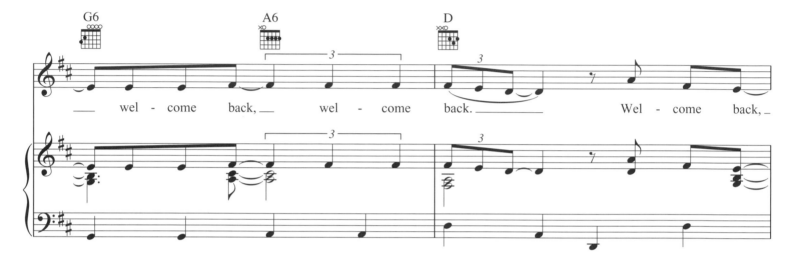

__ wel - come back, __ wel - come back. _____ Wel - come back, __

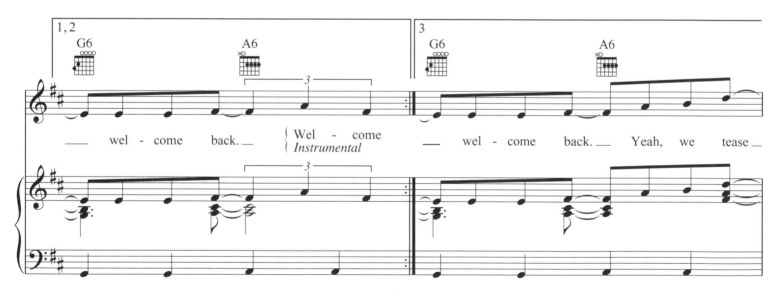

__ wel - come back. __ { Wel - come *Instrumental* __ wel - come back. __ Yeah, we tease __

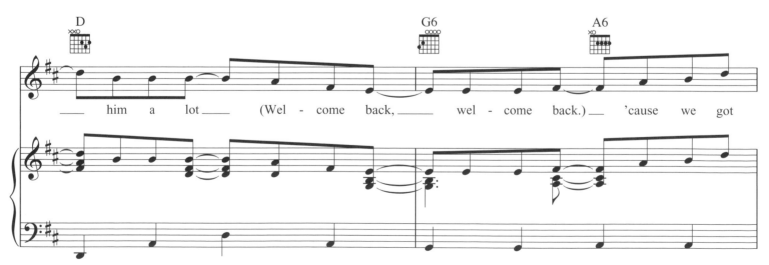

__ him a lot ____ (Wel - come back, ____ wel - come back.) ____ 'cause we got

him on the spot. ___ (Wel - come back, _____ wel - come back.) ___ Yeah, we

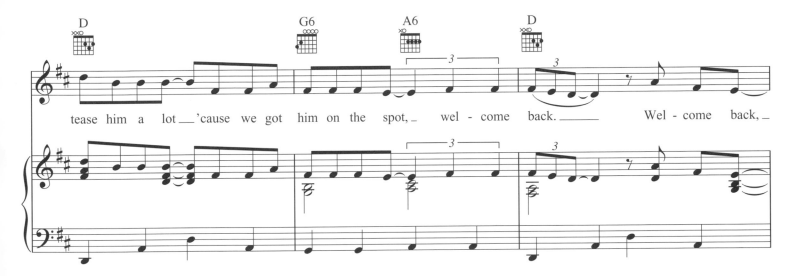

tease him a lot ___ 'cause we got him on the spot, __ wel - come back. _____ Wel - come back, __

___ wel-come back, __ wel - come back. _____ Wel-come back, __ wel-come back, __ wel - come

back. _____ Wel - come back, __ wel - come back, __ wel - come back. _____

YOU'RE A BIG BOY NOW

Words and Music by
JOHN SEBASTIAN

but you're a big boy now. ____ Come on and take a bow ____

To Coda ⊕

'cause you're a big boy now. ____

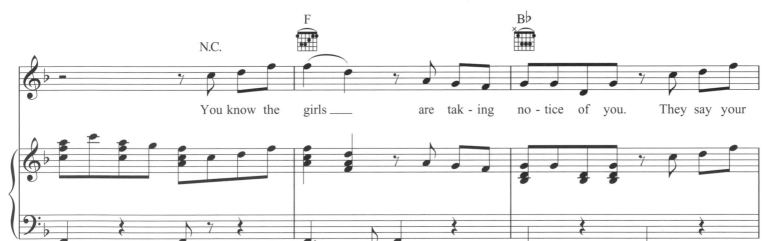

You know the girls ____ are tak-ing no-tice of you. They say your

hair ____ is get-ting curl-y, too. So, shave to-day, ____ you'll shave to-

mor-row as well. __ You're run by you and not a class-room bell, __

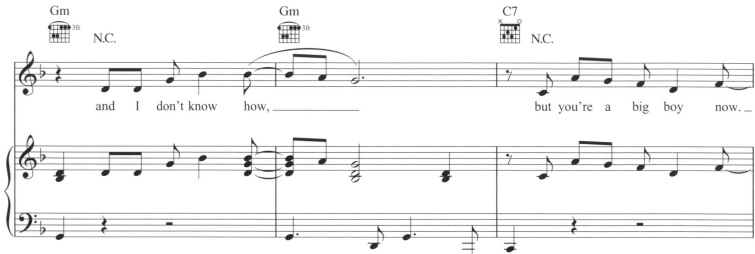

and I don't know how, _____ but you're a big boy now. _

_____ And the great big world __

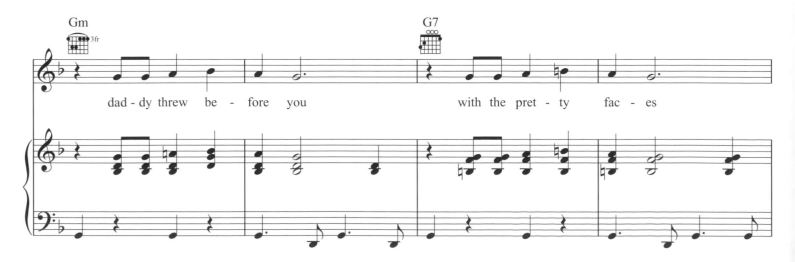

dad-dy threw be-fore you with the pret-ty fac-es

and the claws that tore you and it's all so dif - f'rent

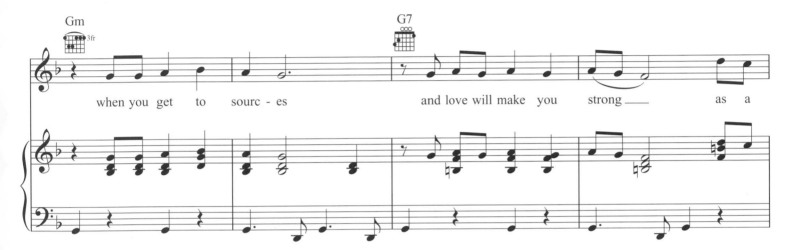

when you get to sourc - es and love will make you strong ___ as a

team of wild ___ hors - es. ___ I know there's

D.S. al Coda

YOUNGER GIRL

Words and Music by
JOHN SEBASTIAN

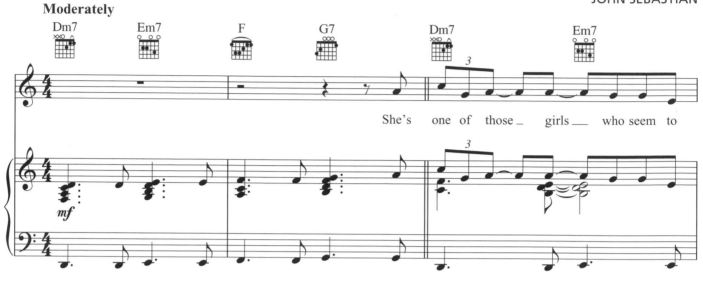

She's one of those __ girls __ who seem to

come in the spring, __ one look in her eyes __ and you for-get ev-'ry-thing __ you had

read-y to say, ___ and I saw her to-day, ___ yeah. __

And a young - er girl ___ keeps roll - in' 'cross ___ my

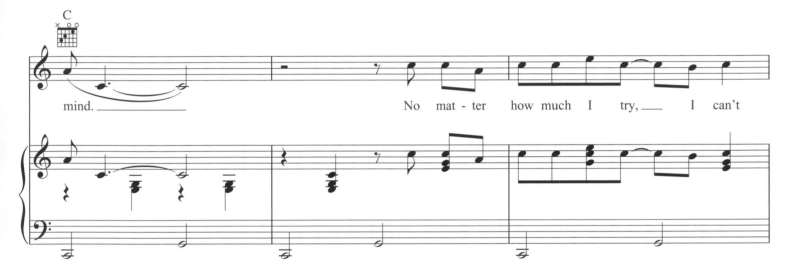

mind. _____ No mat - ter how much I try, ___ I can't

seem to leave her mem - 'ry be - hind. ___ I re -

mem - ber her eyes, ___ soft ___ dark and brown. Said she's nev - er been in trou - ble or

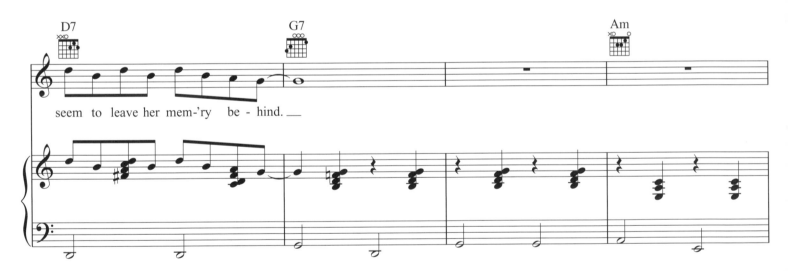

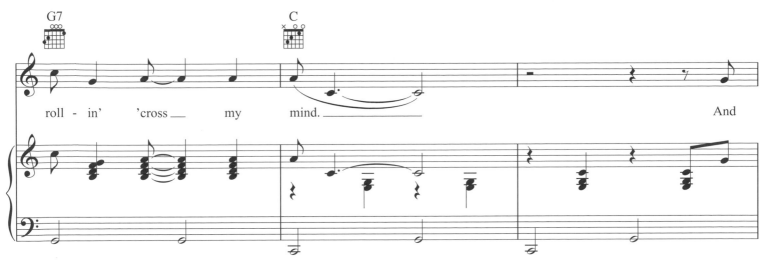

roll - in' 'cross __ my mind. _____ And

should I hang a - round, act - in' like her broth - er? In a few more years __ they'll call us

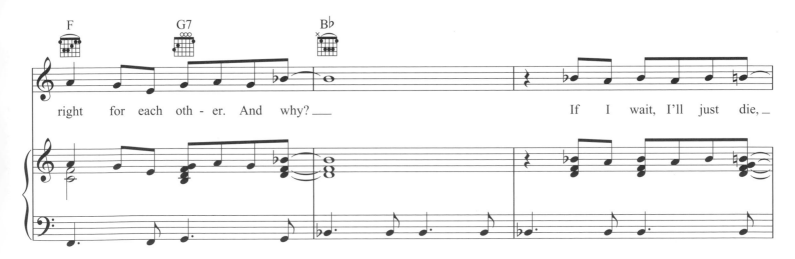

right for each oth - er. And why? __ If I wait, I'll just die, __

D.S. al Coda

yeah. A

CODA